DYN

by George Chung & Cynthia Rothrock

Editor: Mike Lee
Graphic Design: Karen Massad

Art Production: Junko Sadjadpour
Ludovic Szvercsak

Sixth printing 2005

WARNING

This book is presented only as a means of preserving a unique aspect of the heritage of the martial arts. Neither Ohara Publications nor the author makes any representation, warranty or guarantee that the techniques described or illustrated in this book will be safe or effective in any self-defense situation or otherwise. You may be injured if you apply or train in the techniques of self-defense illustrated in this book, and neither Ohara Publications nor the author is responsible for any such injury that may result. It is essential that you consult a physician regarding whether or not to attempt any technique described in this book. Specific self-defense responses illustrated in this book may not be justified in any particular situation in view of all of the circumstances or under the applicable federal, state or local law. Neither Ohara Publications nor the author makes any representation or warranty regarding the legality or appropriateness of any technique mentioned in this book.

BLACK BELT BOOKS
A Division of **OHARA ⓟ PUBLICATIONS, INC.**
World Leader in Martial Arts Publications

Dedication

This book is dedicated to my mother, Joy Markowski, and my father, the late Edward Markowski, who gave me their love and support and who always believed in me. I love you.

—Cynthia

This book is dedicated to my family, and especially to my mother, Yuri Saito, who told her boy he could do anything he wanted in the world if he just believed in himself and never stopped dreaming.

—George

Acknowledgement

From the beginning of this great journey in the martial arts, we have met many people who have taught, inspired, and cared for us. Writing this book, we reflected on the wisdom and value of their teachings, and now would like to thank these special people for being so warm and giving, and salute their excellence: Ernie Reyes, Shum Leung, Roger Tung, Hee Il Cho, Anthony Chan, Frank Trojanowicz, Toshihiro Oshiro, Remy Presas, and Dan K. Choi.

We would like to express a special thanks to Dr. H.N. MacKinnon for his unselfish help, in advising us on the stretching chapter.

And finally, a warm thank you to all of our students at America's Best Martial Arts Academy in Los Gatos, California, and to all our students at Harker Academy in San Jose—thank you for your continued support, loyalty, friendship, and for displaying such character in your pursuit of excellence.

About the Authors

George Chung earned his black belt degree at the age of 15, and is known for, among many other things, introducing contemporary musical forms to martial arts. He was three times the grand champion at the Battle of Atlanta, three times LAMA Nationals grand champion in Chicago, twice Mid-American Diamond Nationals grand champion, U.S. Open grand champion, PKA Nationals grand champion, NKC grand champion, and Fort Worth Pro Am grand champion.

Going beyond his traditional tae kwon do background, Chung has also captured titles in the kung fu, Japanese, Okinawan, and kenpo divisions at many national events. Expert in tae kwon do, karate, wushu, kung fu, and traditional Okinawan kobudo weapons, he has taught students all over North America in many large seminars.

KARATE ILLUSTRATED named him the number one forms champion three times. In 1980 he gained the double crown for being named both number one in forms and number one in weapons, becoming the first male ever to capture both titles in the same year. The only other person ever to have done so was Cynthia Rothrock. In 1983, Chung was inducted into the BLACK BELT Hall of Fame.

Currently, he devotes his full time to running his martial arts center, America's Best, in Los Gatos, California, with his partner Cynthia Rothrock, though his plans include venturing into an acting career in the near future.

As a martial arts competitor, Cynthia Rothrock has captured more championships than any woman in history. Some of these include: the Battle of Atlanta, Mid-American Diamond Nationals, Fort Worth Pro Am, California Superstars Nationals, the Internationals, AKA Grand Nationals, and Century NKC Open Nationals.

In 1982, 1983, and 1984 she went undefeated in every national event she entered in women's forms, winning either first place, or grand champion, a feat yet to be repeated. She was rated number one by KARATE ILLUS-TRATED four times, and became, in 1982, the only woman ever to capture the title of number one in weapons. In 1983 she was inducted into the BLACK BELT Hall of Fame. Rothrock has black belts in kung fu, tae kwon do, tang soo do, and wushu. Her studies have taken her to Hong Kong and the People's Republic of China.

Currently, she devotes her full attention to a successful martial arts school as well as a blossoming acting career. In addition to her instructional videotape, *Defend Yourself*, Cynthia has also appeared in three movies produced by Golden Harvest Films: *Yes, Madam, Noble Express,* and *Armor of God* with martial artist and film star Jackie Chan.

Preface

It is without question the martial arts are a lifetime study. Whether you are in search of self-defense skills, or of developing your physical condition or mental awareness, or just in search of inner peace through this ancient discipline, you are among millions of friends who share a common goal.

For some of you, this book may be a totally new experience; others may find it a useful reference guide—no matter. We all know one thing: we love martial arts. Despite a bump or a bruise, despite discouragement at times, and even defeat, we still return. So, it is for you, the modern-day martial artist, that we wrote this book.

As you read through this book, bear in mind these facts (some will shatter many of your misconceptions about kicking skills):

1. Anyone, regardless of age, size, or experience can become skilled in kicking.

2. You don't need a super-flexible body to become great in kicking. Did you know that three-time national karate champion Keith Vitali (star of the film *Revenge of the Ninja*) has difficulty touching his toes? Even Keith admits, "I'm one of the tighest guys I know." That didn't stop him. And if you ask

him his most successful technique—hook kick to the face!

3. Kicking works in all arenas of the martial arts. It's not just for show. Of course, we all know that some of the very best forms champions were great kickers. But, what about fighters? Well, there is "Superfoot" Bill Wallace, former world middleweight full-contact karate champion. Need we say more?

4. Success will come to those who apply knowledge that has been proven worthy by others, and to those who adhere to the faith that they can and will succeed. There was one woman in Illinois who was 88 when she received her black belt. I guess no one told her she couldn't do it. And of course, there are countless people who became great despite their circumstances: Robert Burns, the great poet, was illiterate; Beethoven, the great composer, was deaf; the list goes on.

Just remember that the open mind takes in everything, and that knowledge is the real power. You are just a few inches from becoming a great success in martial arts. Those few inches are between your ears.

—*G.C. and C.R.*

How to Use this Book

In reading this text, you will discover new insights into some old ways. Read through each chapter carefully, and read all the directions. Don't just glance at the photos. Reading will make the technique easier to understand.

If you come upon a section or chapter that you don't understand, stop; do not pass it up. This way, you don't get into the habit of always passing a difficult section when you get to it. Read through it again and again if necessary; and then, if all else fails, ask for advice. Here is our personal academy address for correspondence, information, or advice with techniques. If you need to, write: America's Best Martial Arts Academy, 442 North Santa Cruz Avenue, Los Gatos, California 95030.

Finally, approach all new ideas with an open mind, and with the willingness to try any new idea once before throwing it out. As the old Zen master said, "Empty your cup before you taste my tea." The same applies here. Release your negative ideas and your past experience. Today marks the beginning of a new adventure. Let's go to it.

The Clock Principle

Here is a method of calling out directions which we use in describing kicking techniques. It relates directions to the face of an imaginary clock.

If the description of a technique reads, "kick from 10:00 o'clock and retract at 2:00 o'clock," then imagine a giant clock in front of your body, the plane of which contains your target. Following the directions, you would kick toward where 10:00 would be on the face of the clock, and recoil your foot across the face of the clock to where 2:00 would be.

This descriptive method will be used in this book to clarify certain kicking techniques.

Contents

POSITIONING

Landing a blow with the wrong area of the foot is usually both injurious as well as ineffective, and so is not positioning your hips properly before full extension. The small bones in your feet can be quite vulnerable, and with the quick snap of the leg that's required in kicking, it's very easy to pull a muscle or worse. When it comes to positioning your kicking foot and leg, always remember that effectiveness and safety go hand in hand.

We cannot overemphasize the importance of making contact with the proper areas of the foot. All of your power will be focused in that small area of your foot. You must make sure that your foot is positioned correctly before contact. And before you extend fully into the kick, make sure your hips are rocked and turned as they should be. This will increase your power and allow your muscles to stretch naturally as you extend.

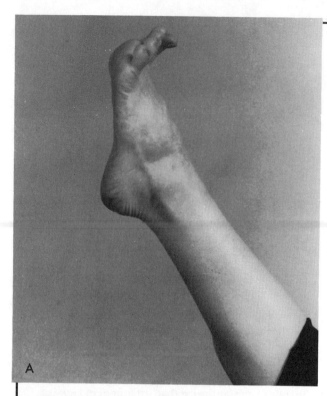

A

Front Kick

Foot Positions

(A) This foot position is for front kicks. Note that contact is made with the ball of the foot, and that the toes are turned up to expose the contact area. (B) For snap kicks, the toes are pointed, and the contact area is the top of the foot. (C) Side kicks are executed with the edge of the foot. The foot is turn-

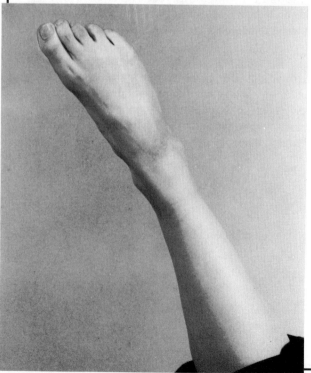

Snap Kick

Side Kick

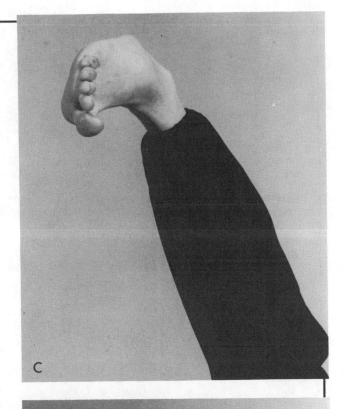

C

ed out at a right angle, and the outside edge, called the knife edge, between the heel and the little toe is the contact area. (D) The heel of the foot is used in axe kicks. Here the whole foot is angled up so that the heel makes contact when the leg is forcefully lowered on the target.

Axe Kick

D

Hip Position
for Front Kick, Round Kick,
Crescent Kick, Axe Kick

The standard way of executing this hip position is (1) assume a guard position, then (2) bring your rear leg up and forward with knee bent and toward the target. Keep your shoulders and hips squared with the target. (2A) For fighting a modified position is used in which the shoulders and hips rare turned slightly toward the target.

1

Hip Position
for Side Kick, Hook Kick

(1) From your guard position, (2) slide your rear foot up directly behind your lead foot, then (3) raise your lead leg in a tucked position by rocking your body back slightly and swinging your lead hip toward the target.

1

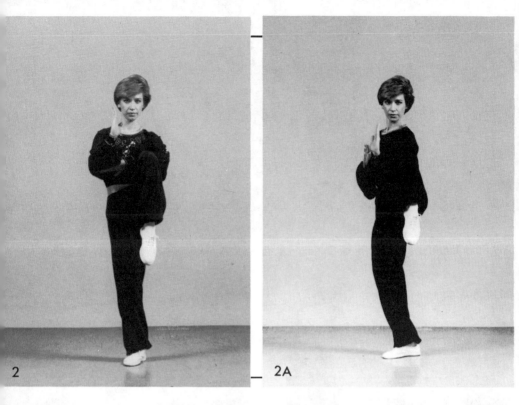

2   2A

2   3

WARM-UP STRETCHING

Stretching is our beginning and our end. Using it, we train successfully; not using it, we painfully regret our very participation in this discipline of martial arts. Stretching increases the circulation of blood in those areas being stretched, supplying more oxygen to the muscles, and increasing stamina. Elongating the muscles also releases much of the tension in them, causing less strain, and also increasing stamina. But, just as importantly, stretching is an exercise in beginning things correctly, and is invaluable for this element of discipline it brings to our training.

Always start from the head and work down. Take each exercise slowly, and gradually increase the number of repetitions as you become more flexible. Do not bounce or jerk. Rather, hold each position and elongate. This is referred to as static stretching. Often, we use another term as well—"pulse." Pulsing means moving a small distance steadily and easily to create a pull and tension wave as gentle as the pulsing of your heart.

This chapter names the muscles specifically for a more refined understanding, but in more general terms: the latissimus dorsi muscles are those broad back muscles that give your torso its V shape; the external oblique are at the sides of your torso; the lumbar muscles are in the lower back; the sartorius runs diagonally from the hip bone, across the front, to the inside of your thigh; the quadriceps are in the front thigh region; the bicep femoris is the hamstring; the gastrocnemius is the calf muscle; and the soleus muscles are located along the inside and outside of the lower leg. In addition, abductors are any muscles used to spread the limbs outward, and adductors are any that pull the limbs inward.

Side Stretch

The first warm-up is essential for loosening up your sides, shoulders, arms, and back. The muscles that are benefitted most are: the latissimus dorsi, the external oblique, and lumbar muscles. Keeping one hand on the hip, lift the opposite hand overhead, keeping your toes pointed in the direction of the stretch. Make sure that your body stays in complete side alignment to insure maximum benefits; and perform the stretch with a slight pulse (a rhythmic bouncing motion extending to the limit of the stretch and coming back from it slightly). Do a set of three repetitions for one side and then reverse sides and do another set. Alternating in this way, do five sets per side.

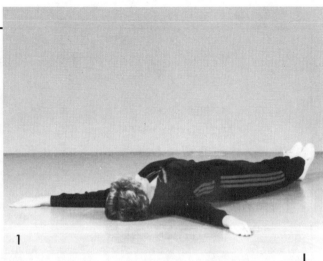

Back Release

This exercise helps increase flexibility in the lower back, lumbar region. Those with weak backs should do it slowly and with caution. (1) Lying on your back in a relaxed state, (2) bring your knee up, and (3) cross it over to the other side of your body. Hold for five seconds and release. Then alternate sides, doing five sets per side.

Upper Torso Stretch

This is an overall upper torso stretch. Almost all muscles are benefited: latissimus dorsi, lumbar, and also the bicep femoris and gastrocnemius muscles located in the back of the leg. As you go through all the positions, hold each one for at least three to five seconds. (1) Standing in a relaxed position with your legs slightly more than shoulder distance apart, interlock your fingers and (2) raise them above your head. (3) Slowly stretch to the side, keeping your body in a complete side position. (4) Alternate sides. (5) Coming back up to a vertical position with hands overhead, (6&7) stretch for-

Continued

ward. (8) Slowly reach with one hand for the opposite ankle. (9) Release and with the other hand, grab the ankle of its opposite side. (10) Hold both ankles and pull through the center. To increase the stretch, (11) put your hands behind your head. Repeat for a total of five sets.

1

Ankle to Toe Flex

This exercise is excellent for developing and stretching the bicep femoris (commonly referred to as the hamstring) and the gastrocnemius. (1) Begin with your hands at your sides and feet apart. (1A) Be sure to keep a firm lower abdomen but not too tense. (2) Shift your weight to one leg, and extend the other foot to the front with toes pointing upward. Extend you elbow forward at shoulder level. (2A) Flex your support leg so that you can lower your body even more if necessary. (3) Bend forward and touch your elbow to your toes, keeping your other hand in a fist at your hip. (3A) Some of your weight will naturally shift to your forward heel, but the majority is still settled on your back leg which should remain flexed at all times. Do this exercise for both sides alternately, holding each side for 15-30 seconds; and complete four sets for each side.

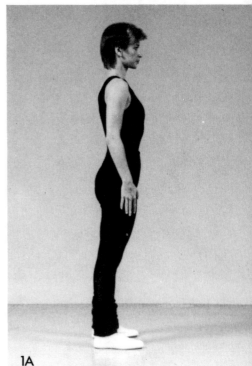

Side View

1A

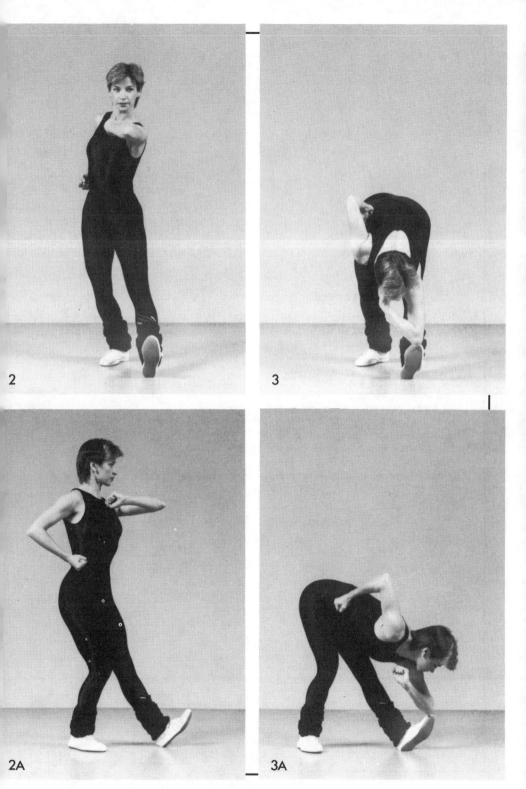

2

3

2A

3A

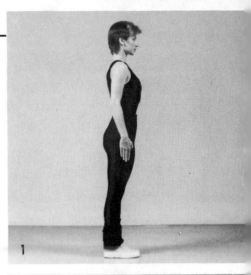

Drop Stance Stretch

The muscles benefited by this exercise are: the sartorius, bicep femoris, gastrocnemius, and soleus. (1) Starting from a standing position, (2) step forward with your left leg. Lunge forward, feeling the stretch in the quadricep. (3) Bring your chest to your knee, and hold. Now, (4&5) straighten your left leg out as far as you can. (6) Lift your toes, and feel the stretch in your calf and hamstring. (7&8) Sit down on your right leg with the knee out at a 45-degree angle. Repeat the exercise for the other side. Alternating sides, complete three to five repetitions per side.

1

Standing Leg Balance ("The Roth Rock")

This exercise improves not only your flexibility but also your balance and above all, your concentration. (1) Starting from a still position, grasp the bottom of your

2

3

foot, and (2-4) slowly raise it overhead to as vertical a position as you can, extending to the limit of your own full extension. Repeat the exercise for the other leg.

4

Hip Flex

This exercise benefits the hip muscles (gluteus medius) and is excellent for developing your side kick. (1) Sitting down, bring your foot to the inside of your thigh. (2) Bring the other leg over to the opposite side, place your foot flat on the ground. Holding your knee stationary with your arms, turn your chest toward your knee, hold, and feel the stretch. If you don't feel the stretch, pull your knee closer to your chest. Then, do the other side. Hold this stretch position for at least ten seconds for each side. Alternating from side to side, do five for each side.

Rothrock's Famous Front Splits

This exercise stretches the femoris, gastrocnemius, and soleus. Holding the stretch position benefits your balance and power. (1) Lower yourself carefully into a front split. Keep your legs straight. No matter how far you can go, feel the stretch and hold. (2) As a variation to the exercise for those who are very flexible, reach back with one hand, and pull your rear foot up toward your torso.

Straddle Splits (Chung Splits)

This exercise again has many variations. It develops stretch throughout your legs, helping and benefiting all your kicks. The muscles that are developed are: adductors, abductors, bicep femoris, gastrocnemius, as well as upper torso groups such as lattissimus dorsi. With a slight pulse, hold each position for at least five seconds. (1) Starting from a sitting position, spread your legs as far apart as you can. (2) Raise your arms overhead, (3&4) keeping your alignment straight, bring one hand to the opposite toe while you rest the other in the center. (5&6) Alternate and work the other side. (7) Come back to the center and bringing your chest toward the floor, stretch your arms out in front. (8) Then, swing your torso over to one side, grabbing hold of your foot to pull yourself further into the stretch. (9) Swing to the other side and do the same. Complete the entire routine at least five times.

4

7

Super Stretch

This exercise develops both biceps femoris as well as adductors. The balance and flexibility required by this drill are extreme. (1) Standing with your heels to a wall, lean forward, putting your palms on the floor while you raise one leg in a bent position up against the wall. (2) Then straighten your leg for the stretch, and hold for ten seconds. Then alternate legs.

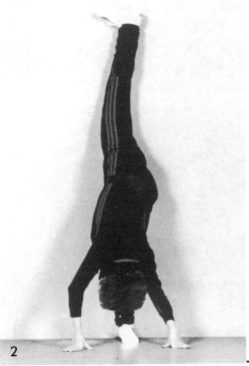

Double Butterfly Stretch

This exercise helps increase flexibility in the adductors, the area needed for side kicking. (1) Assume the butterfly stretch position by putting the soles of your feet together and bringing your feet up to as close to your body as you can. (2) Your parnter kneels in front of you. (3) As you lay back, your partner presses down both your thighs toward the floor. Hold for five-ten seconds with a very light pulse, and repeat for five sets.

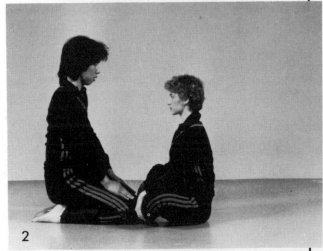

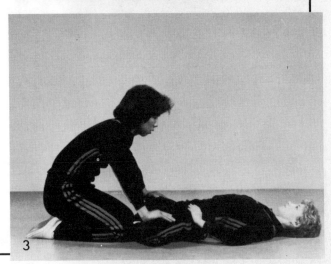

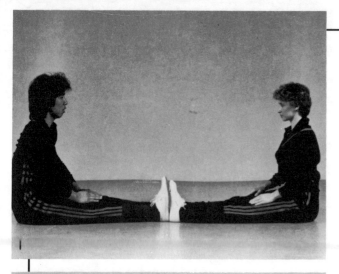

Toe to Toe Stretch

This exercise benefits the biceps femoris. (1) Sitting across from each other, place the soles of your feet together. (2&3) Reach toward each other and hold hands. Stretch each other by one of you leaning back, forcing the other to lean forward into the stretch, hold for five seconds and then alternate. Do five sets each.

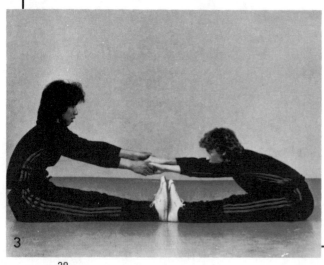

Front Kick Stretch

This exercise will stretch out the biceps femoris as well as the sartorius. The extra help from your partner will push you beyond normal limits. (1) Stand with your back against a wall. (2) Raise your leg as high as you can, keeping your knee straight. (3) Have your partner lift your leg higher for the maximum stretch.

Side Kick Stretch

To develop the stretch for your side kick position, (1) stand with one hand resting on the back of a chair for support. Extend your leg out to the side as if executing a high side kick, and have a partner support your foot in that position. (2) Your partner walks in as you withdraw your foot into the cocked side kick position. Your partner exerts force on your foot until you feel the stretch. (3&4) Repeat the same procedure for a midsection side kick, having your partner support your foot at a midsection level, then walk in toward you to exert pressure for the stretch.

Back and Quadriceps Stretch

For the more advanced and flexible, this exercise will develop the back and also the sartorius and front thigh muscle region, or quadriceps. (1) Using your partner's arm for support, (2) balance on one leg and raise one foot up behind you. Your partner supports your raised leg with his other hand. (3) With your partner's assistance, raise your foot up toward the back of your head as far as you can to your full extension.

1

2

3

Side Stretch

This exercise develops flexibility in the adductors. The stretch is really a side kick held and pushed higher. (1) Resting one hand against the wall for support, assume the side kick position. (2) Then, as your partner lifts your leg higher, be sure to keep your hips tucked and your back straight.

Two Man Exercise for Power

Dynamic tension is a very good way to develop power in your kicks. This technique uses the controlled resistance of your partner throughout the kicking action. (1&2) With your partner at the proper kicking distance, (2) raise your foot into the front kick position against your partner's stomach. (3&4) Slowly extend your leg in the same motion you would perform a front kick except slowly. Your partner pushes back against your leg hard enough to make your extension difficult but not impossible. It should take three-five seconds to fully extend your kick. Repeat the exercise ten times for each leg. (5-7) Next, assume the side kick position and repeat the same procedure for the side kick, also ten times for each leg.

1

4

5

2

3

6

7

Leg Workout

This exercise is tremendous for developing explosive power in all kicking techniques that require leg strength. It also improves your timing by making you quicker in the legs. (1) Standing back to back, (2&3) interlock your arms at the elbows, and slowly start to sit down all the way to the floor. (4) Extend your legs out, then (5-8) return to a standing position slowly.

Roundhouse Flex

The use of a belt makes this exercise very interesting and useful. (1) Using a knot that will not cut off your circulation, tie a belt around one ankle. Have your partner hold the other end as he kneels beside you on the floor. Lay on your side with the other leg extended out and your tied leg cocked in the ready position at a 45-

degree angle. (2&3) Extend your leg out slowly in the kicking motion while your partner pulls back on the belt to make your slow kick difficult but not impossible. Then, (4&5) return to the starting position. Take five seconds for your full extension, but do not apply any tension on the return. Do ten repetitions for each leg.

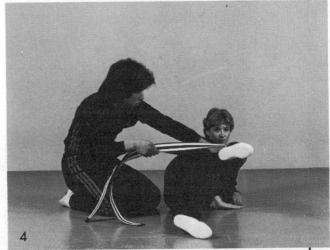

BASIC KICKS

All great adventures start with one step. This is true in kicking as well, for indeed, it will be a great adventure. Basic kicks from the ground, that is, kicks performed from a standing position without jumping, skipping, or spinning, are the prerequisite for your success in all aspects of kicking. Remember as you execute these kicks, to practice each technique with the focus, speed, power and intent of the actual situation. Practice does not make perfect. Perfect practice makes perfect. Train with that in mind.

Front Kick

(1) Begin in a guard position, hands held high. (2) Bring your knee forward and up, bent sharply, toes pulled back. (3) Thrust the kick forward, hitting with the ball of the foot. Tense your thigh and buttocks upon impact, then (4) recoil your foot, and (5) return to the guard stance position. *Tips for a great kick:* Keep your back straight. Don't bend forward. A bent body position will hinder the height of the kick. Keep your eyes on the target always, and exhale on impact.

5

Rear Leg Side Kick

(1) Begin in a guard stance, hands held up. (2) Bring your rear leg up as high as you can, and pivot your back foot in the opposite direction. This is essential for a great kick. (3) Thrust out your foot, striking with the heel or the knife edge. Tense your buttocks and thighs at the moment of impact. (4) Recoil to the chambered position. (5) Settle back to your guard stance. *Tips for a great kick:* The pivot is first in line of importance. A good pivot will enhance the power of your kick. Secondly, the higher you kick, the higher you will need to bring your chamber. The chamber in a high position will also enable you to block out any counter techniques to the body with your knee such as reverse punches. Lastly, if you are having difficulty achieving height, try leaning your body slightly; however, when leaning back, keep your head up, as this will keep you from losing balance and falling.

1

3

54

Basic Roundhouse

(1) Begin in a guard stance with your hands held high. (2) Chamber your leg forward at a 45-degree angle, and pivot your bottom foot. (3) Extend your kicking leg, and strike with the ball of the foot. (4) Recoil the foot back to the chambered position, and (5) return to your guard stance. *Tips for a great kick:* The roundhouse kick is best thrown when you execute it in a circular motion, hips turned out. A slight overextension of the target range is necessary to insure that you strike your target with power. This is due to the fact that the basic roundhouse is a shorter-distanced kick than most others.

1

3

2

4

5

Slide Up Hook Kick: Face of the Foot

(1) Begin with a guard position stance. (2) Bring up the rear leg next to your front leg. (3) Chamber the knee at a 45-degree angle, making sure the knee is up high to protect against a body attack. Pivot the back foot as well. (4) Begin the kick outward, and at full peak, immediately (5) recoil. This action gives you that snap that you need for a powerful kick. (6) Recoil back to the chambered position, and (7) resume your fighting stance. *Tips for a great kick:* The most common error with the hook kick is not bringing the foot around to the proper position for striking the target. Visualize this: a large clock in front of you. When you kick, begin by kicking at 10:00 o'clock, and finish the kick, the impact point, at 2:00 o'clock; vice versa for the left leg. The face of this imaginary clock places your target within a plane. Because your initial move is not directly toward the target, judging your kicking distance can be a problem. This imaginary plane helps you establish the proper distance in applying the hook kick.

1

3

6

2

4

5

7

Outside Crescent Kick:
Knife Edge

(1) Begin in the forward stance guard position. (2) Start your back leg up in a circular motion to the opposite side of your kicking hip. (3) Begin the kick upward, remembering the circular motion of your action. (4) Peak the kick at 12:00 o'clock, and (5) start your return to your original position as soon as the leg drops to shoulder level. (6) Return to your guard position. *Tips for a great kick:* Once again, visualize the clock in front of you. Start the kick at 9:00 o'clock, bring it up to 10:00 o'clock, peak at 12:00 o'clock and return to 2:00 o'clock; and vice versa for the opposite side. Momentum is the key to this kick. Use your hips to generate power by using a slight twist before full peak.

1

4

Inside Crescent Kick:
Knife Edge and Face of the Foot

(1) Begin in your guard stance, hands held high. (2) Start your kick by bringing it around to the outside. (3) Begin to bring the kick to the inside of your body in a circular motion. (4) Impact is made at 1:00 o'clock or 11:00 o'clock, depending on which leg is kicking. (5) The striking of the hand symbolizes the target. (6) Return to your guard position. Remember to keep your leg straight throughout the kick. *Tips for a great kick:* If you kick with your right leg, bring the kick to 9:00 o'clock, then up to 11:00 o'clock, impact at 1:00 o'clock, and return after 3:00. The kick is best done when your body is as straight as possible. This will insure good posture and maximum extension on impact.

1

4

1

Axe Kick

This kick is similar to the outside crescent kick. Imagine your target directly under the 12:00 o'clock mark as you (1) begin in your fighting stance. (2&3) Lift your kicking leg to the outside shoulder of your opponent. If you kick with your right leg, raise it to the outside of his right shoulder, 11:00 o'clock. If you kick with your left, raise it to the outside of his left shoulder, 1:00 o'clock. (4&5) Peak your kicking leg at 12:00 o'clock, and (6&7) forcefully drive down with your heel or with the face of your foot into the target. Impact can be made to the head or the chest, and then (8) return to your fighting stance. *Tips for a great kick:* This kick relies upon complete accuracy. The momentum for the kick is gained as your leg is coming down, not going up. Use your hips to thrust slightly downward; however, keep your head forward to maintain your balance and keep from falling back.

3

6

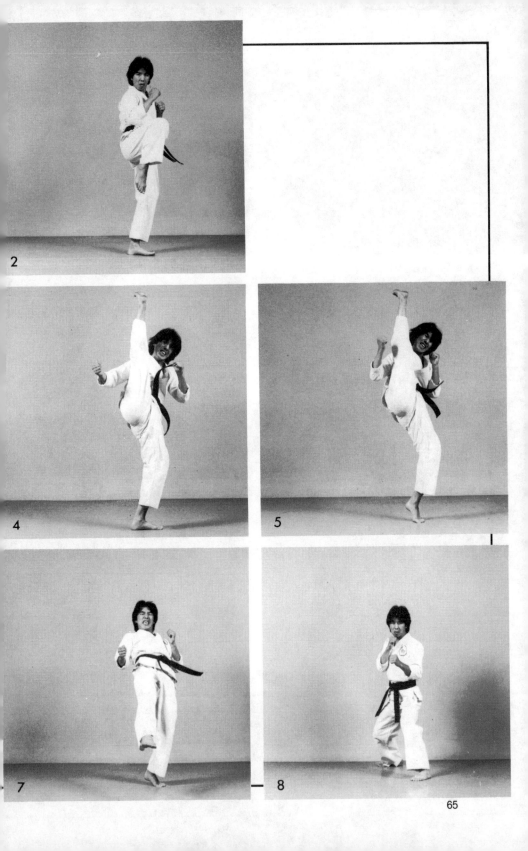

SPINNING KICKS

With the perfection of the basic kicks, your next step toward achieving kicking mastery is learning the spinning kick. But, two great dangers accompany the spinning kick, and they must never be overlooked. The technique requires that you turn your back to your opponent for one brief moment. And, more than most kicks, the spinning kick can cause you to lose balance.

The advantages, however, far outweigh the disadvantages. An extraordinary amount of power is generated by the turn; and the characteristic sudden shift in the angle of attack obtains for you an element of surprise which very often spells victory.

Spin kicking emerged in sport tournaments when movie star and karate legend Chuck Norris introduced it during his fabulous reign as world champion. Many world full-contact fighters use spinning kicks in the ring as well, and to great advantage.

Famed tae kwon do expert Hee Il Cho has made spin kicking his stock and trade to become one of the most celebrated martial artists in the world.

To become proficient in it, remember to break the kick down step by step before you try full execution. This will insure your complete understanding of the technique, and enable you to maintain your balance. Take the kick slowly at first until you become more comfortable with the motion. Later, with confidence, you can increase your speed and shorten that moment during which your back is turned. But don't give up. The result of the spin kick can be devastating.

Spin Back Kick:
Heel or Knife Edge

(1) Begin in your fighting stance, right leg back. (2) Turn your body half around, and turn your head sharply to spot your target over your shoulder. (3&4) Chamber your right leg to a side thrust position at a 45-degree angle. As you continue turning your body, kick. At impact, tense your thighs and buttocks, and continue in that pattern forward. Bring your leg back to a chambered position, and (5) return to a fighting stance. *Tips for a great kick:* The most common mistake occurs with body position. Most people dip toward the floor as they kick. This does two things: first, it takes your focus away from your target; second, it counters your body to an off-balance position. Keep your back straight and head forward. Turn quickly to eliminate the risk of no sight, and extend to your full range, and recoil.

1

3

2

4

5

1

Spin Hook Kick

This kick is often referred to as the spin-ning wheel kick. (1) Start with your hands held high in the fighting stance. (2) Start your kick again just like the spin turn back kick, looking over your shoulder of the kicking leg. (3) Chamber your knee to a 45-degree angle. (4) Begin the hook kick, reaching your leg from 10:00 o'clock to the full locked-out position, (5) hitting with the face of the foot. At impact, tighten the area of contact. (6) Chamber through to 2:00 o'clock, and return to the fighting stance. *Tips for a great kick:* Think of your body as a whirl-wind when executing this kick. Momentum is the key, as well as speed, and the full extension from 10:00 o'clock to 2:00 o'clock. Remember, with spinning kicks, it is best to initiate your attack with a safe kick, then follow through with the spin. However, this kick is also effective used right off your opponent's attack.

3

6

2

4

5

7

Spin Outside Crescent Kick: Knife Edge

(1) Start from a fighting stance. (2) Look over your shoulder as you turn your body. (3) Begin to lift your leg straight up. Notice the clock again to note the angle from which you start your kick. Keep your leg straight until it reaches peak extension. Begin to bring the leg back, and return to the guard position. *Tips for a great kick:* Keeping your leg straight at all times is very important in this kick. The power is developed through the momentum of your body spin. Make sure your head is up, and your body is not bent too far forward.

2

4

5

7

8

JUMP KICKS

It's natural to be hesitant about going into the air to execute a kick since once you've left the ground, you're committed. But, with practice, you'll gain confidence, and your initial apprehension will simply become good judgment. Then, you'll look forward to the opportunity to score with a jump kick.

Jump kick techniques start with the mastery of basic ground kicks and spinning kicks. Since most of your hip and leg positioning takes place in the air, you must already have developed the skill at being quick about it, having perfected these actions on the ground.

When you come down, do it softly. Land first on the balls of your feet, then the soles of your feet, and then be sure to flex your knees. This will cushion your landing and help to prevent injury.

Pop-Up Front Kick

(1) Begin in your fighting stance. (2) Jump up, bringing your rear leg forward toward the target, knee bent sharply. (3) Extend the kick, hitting with the ball of the foot. At the moment of impact, tense your thigh and buttocks for maximum power. (4) Relax and start the recoil, (5&6) landing on your opposite leg, and returning to your fighting stance. *Tips for a great kick:* Pop-up kicks, because of their multiple action, require speed and endurance. Make sure you are properly stretched before you attempt any such actions. Remember when landing, land on the balls of your feet rather than the heels. This will absorb the landing better. Also, try to keep your head forward to insure better balance when you land.

1

4

2

3

5

6

Pop-Up Side Kick

(1) Begin in your fighting stance. (2) Jump straight up, bringing your front leg up at a 45-degree angle. Your hips will turn slightly at this point. (3) Execute the side kick, hitting with the knife edge or heel. Tense your thighs and buttocks at the point of impact. (4) Recoil back to the chamber, (5) land, and settle back into your fighting stance. *Tips for a great kick:* It is important when executing the pop-up side kick that you bring your knees up as high as you can. When you execute, also keep your hips pulled in and your back straight. This will increase the impact.

1

3

2

4

5

Pop-Up Roundhouse

(1) Begin in your fighting stance. (2&3) Jump up, bringing your rear leg all the way to the front of your body at a 45-degree angle. (4) Execute, hitting with the ball of the foot. Note the position of the hips. Here they are stuck out for the circular effect and application. (5) Recoil the leg back to the chambered position, and (6) land with your kicking leg forward, resuming your fighting stance. *Tips for a great kick:* The pop-up roundhouse is great for close range. Like the basic roundhouse, it has a short extension, however, due to its circular motion, it generates a great deal of power. Remember not to bring your arms up to begin the initial jump. This is a common error for beginners when they try to get more altitude in the jump. Throwing your arms up before striking opens your body up and makes it vulnerable to attack.

1

4

2

3

5

6

Pop-Up Back Kick

(1) Begin in a fighting stance. You will execute the kick with your rear foot. To do this, (2) leap straight up, turning your body 180 degrees to the right if you kick with your right leg, and 180 degrees to the left if you kick with your left leg. Quickly turn your head to spot your target over your shoulder as you tuck up your kicking leg at a 45-degree angle, bringing your knee as high as you can. (3) Execute, hitting with the edge or heel of the foot. (4) As you begin to recoil, (5) chamber your leg back. (6) Settle down again into your fighting stance, kicking leg forward. *Tips for a great kick:* The pop-up back kick is a very powerful kick. One reason is the spin for momentum. Remember to bring your legs up and chamber your knee very tightly. This will generate more speed in your spin. As you kick, your head turns and your eyes focus almost at the same time of impact. Also, keep your arms in tight. The open-arm fighter will be thrown off like an unbalanced helicopter. Lastly, keep your head straight up to ensure balance.

1

4

2

3

5

6

Pop-Up Hook Kick

This kick is similar to the pop-up side kick in execution. (1) From a fighting stance, (2) jump, and raise your leg to the chambered position at a 45-degree angle. Then, like the basic hook kick, follow the clock pattern, (3) starting at 10:00 o'clock, and (4) going across to 2:00 o'clock to strike with the face of the foot or the heel. (5&6) Recoil and return to your fighting position. *Tips for a great kick:* The pop-up hook kick must be a very spontaneous kick. In order to strike with it effectively, you must not telegraph your intentions with any preliminary movement. Once again, keep your head forward to ensure better balance as you land.

1

4

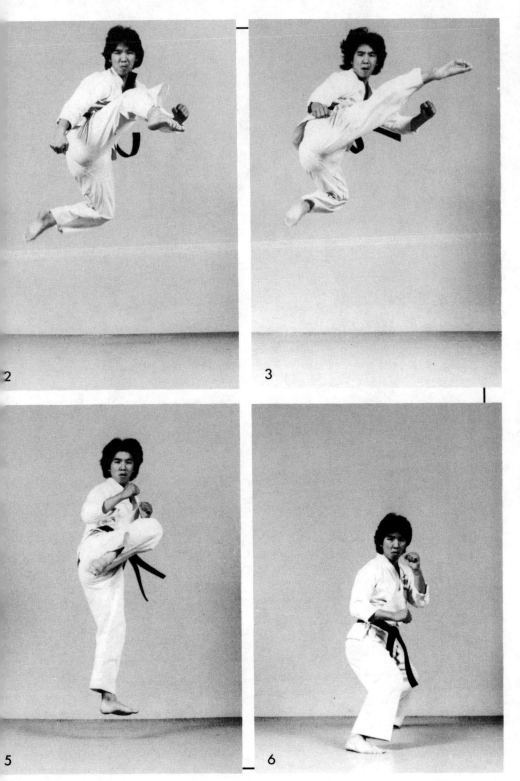

2

3

5

6

FLYING KICKS

The term "flying kicks" refers to jump kicks executed with a running approach. The approach increases the critical nature of perfecting your jump kick technique. If something is wrong with your jump kick, the flying kick version will betray you with a vengeance, all because of the very qualities which are virtues of the flying kick—increased height and increased body momentum. So, be sure that your jump kicks are highly polished, from take off to landing.

The buddy, or spotter method described in this chapter will help your flying kicks tremendously and with less risk of injury. Remember also to keep your eyes ahead and your mind alert. You want all phases of this technique to be perfect.

Running Jump Front Kick

(1) From your fighting stance, (2) step forward with your rear leg, the kicking leg. This is considered the approach. (3) Lift your other knee as high as you can, and before your raised knee comes down, push off with your kicking leg, leaping into the air. (4) Execute the front kick with your kicking leg while in the air, striking with the ball of the foot. (5) Recoil your kicking leg, and (6) land gently back into your fighting stance. *Tips for a great kick:* On the jump front kick, you may take more steps than are illustrated here, however, make sure your last two match these. Try to keep your back straight and your head forward. This will keep you on balance. On landing, make sure you land with the balls of the feet first, then settle to the heels. The balls of the feet will act as shock absorbers against rough landings.

1

4

1

Training for the
Flying Side Kick
(Spotter Method)

To help develop your jumping ability, some special training methods have been included for use in perfecting your technique. Initially, your fear of landing badly can cause you to lose the polish of your side kick technique in the air. This method will accustom you to following through with good technique while in the air. (1) Begin with your partner standing behind you. (2) Your partner holds you by your waist as you both flex your knees in preparation for the jump.

2

(3) Your partner lifts you as you jump into the air and rock your hips to the proper side kick position. (4) At the peak of your jump, execute your side kick. With your partner's support, you will remain in the air a moment longer than you would on your own, allowing you to give your full attention to executing correctly, and getting the feel of the flying side kick done correctly. When you do it on your own, be sure to get the same feel in the technique.

3

4

Flying Side Kick

(1) From the fighting stance, (2&3) take two steps forward for your approach. On the second step, plant your takeoff leg with a slight inverted step, and (4) lift both legs up together and tuck your knees tightly to your chest. (5) Execute the side kick. There are two ways to execute the flying side kick, one with your back leg tucked and the other with it straight. (6) Recoil your leg back to the chambered position, and (7) land softly into the fighting stance. *Tips for a great kick:* Once again, you may take as many steps as you like before the kick. Just make sure to follow the same approach before takeoff. This kick is very beautiful as well as effective when done correctly. Make sure your head is forward for balance on the landing. Also, keep your eyes on the target during the entire technique focus. It is difficult when striking in the air, but setting up targets for practice will help to develop a better kick. They will also motivate you to a higher kick if you raise them to progressively higher levels.

2

4

5

7

Training for the
Jump Back Kick
(Spotter and Hurdle Method)

The spotter and hurdle method will enhance your jumping ability by giving you
a better idea of what the actual jump
back kick will feel like at full air position.
(1) To begin, your partner crouches with
his hands resting above his knees to
support his upper body. (2) You approach from one side, and (3) by using
your partner's lower back as support, (4)
leap into the air while your partner rises
up slightly to further aid your leap. (5) Execute the jump back kick with your legs,
using your partner for support in the air.
This support keeps you in the air longer
and allows you to coordinate your move-
ments consciously and overcome the initial disorientation of the spin. This will
give you a good idea of what a full jump
back kick should feel like.

2

4

5

Jump Back Kick

(1) From your fighting stance, (2) bring your back leg forward and up as you would for a roundhouse kick, except (3) follow through by using the momentum of your rising leg to help you push off with the other leg, your kicking leg. (4&5) Execute the back kick by spinning your body around rapidly and striking with the heel of the same foot with which you pushed off the ground. (6) Recoil the leg back to the chambered position. (7) Land gently back into the fighting stance.

1

4

5

2

3

6

7

Jump Spinning Wheel Kick

(1) Begin with your fighting stance. (2) Bring your rear leg forward and up forcefully, giving your body an upward impetus as you (3) push off with your other foot, your kicking foot. (4) At the peak of your jump, spin to bring your pushoff leg up and around to hook kick with the face of the foot. (5) The momentum of this kick is very great and should bring your kicking leg back to the original starting position as you recoil and land. *Tips for a great kick:* This is a very difficult kick and should not be attempted until you have just about perfected the hook kick and wheel kick. Once again, keep your head forward and straight ahead.

5

Jump Inside Crescent Kick

(1) This kick begins in a crane stance. (2) As you drop your raised leg down, (3) step forward with the other leg into a horse stance. Then, immediately (4) lift your back leg straight up forcefully to give your body an upward impetus as you (5) push off with your forward leg which will execute the kick. (6) Swing your pushoff leg up and around to execute the crescent kick, striking with the inside of your foot. (7) Follow through on the kick, allowing your momentum to turn your body back to (8) your original horse stance.

2

4

5

7

8

Jump Outside Crescent Kick

(1) Start this technique from a high standing cat stance with hands held in a double knife hand block. You can alter your hand position, however, your feet should be in the same position. (2) Step further out with your lead foot into a forward stance, and (3) then take a complete step forward, twisting your body as you plant your foot. (4&5) Push off with that foot, lifting your back leg up forcefully to give yourself an upward impetus as you continue your spin in the

2

4

5

Continued

air. (6) Execute the outside crescent kick with your pushoff leg, (7) striking with the outside edge of your foot, and (8) slapping your hand to your foot. (9&10) Land gently and immediately (11) assume a fighting stance. *Tips for a great kick:* This is a very difficult kick to develop if you don't start out with the basic kicks first. You must have perfected the outside crescent kick. Also, keep your back straight and your head high to maintain better balance throughout. This kick must be done in one continuous motion, and it is even more difficult to do it slowly. Momentum is the key to it. If you find yourself going backwards a bit, that's okay; it's part of the technique.

6

9

7

8

10

11

MACHINE GUN KICKS

Machine gun kicks are the final step in putting our complete kicking system together. At the heart of this technique, and at the heart of the kicking system, is feeling. Of course, all the basics must be there, the proper training described in previous chapters, the proper attitude of giving it all you've got, the proper physical condition of well-trained muscles that are thoroughly stretched and warmed up. You are the reflection of your own hard work.

But, the rapid-fire speed of machine gun kicks requires a special state of mind we call relaxed intensity. On the one hand, the body stays loose and warm, but on the other, the mind is sharp and alert. In this state of mind, your body feels as if it is building a reserve of energy along with a bit of ner-vousness. You are familiar with this nervousness, you know it won't stop you, but is simply there to hold your energy, the way a trigger holds back the firing pin of a gun.

You must see yourself as very fast. Visualize being so fast that only a blur will be seen by others. You must convince yourself that you are indeed fast before you can be fast. Then let go, pull the trigger and move, move fast like a machine gun. And when the smoke clears, you'll be standing there feeling as if the clouds were under your feet.

Fake Front Kick Roundhouse

(1) Begin from a fighting stance. (2) Bring your back knee forward and up so it appears as a front kick attempt. (3) Extend your foot forward so it goes into a half kick. (4) Immediately recoil it to rise into the 45-degree hip position for the roundhouse. (5) Execute the roundhouse, and (6) return your leg back to the chambered position, and then (7) let it down. *Tips for a great kick:* When doing this technique, set it up first by throwing a couple of front kicks at your opponent. This will give him the impression you are a front kicking fighter. As your opponent tries to block and counter your kick, execute the fake front kick and go upstairs with the roundhouse. Remember not to extend the fake front kick too far, just enough to get your opponent to react.

1

4

5

Double Roundhouse

(1) Begin this kick from a fighting stance. (2) As you slide your back foot up directly behind your lead foot, rock your hips into the roundhouse position. (3) Execute a low roundhouse aimed for the shin area of your opponent. (4) Then, immediately recoil your leg back and rock your hips for a higher roundhouse. (5&6) Execute a high roundhouse to the head. (7) Bring your leg back to the chambered position, and (8) return to your fighting stance. *Tips for a great kick:* This technique requires good timing as all multiple machine gun kicks do. Sometimes you may want to pause a moment longer before you bring the second kick up; or perhaps a fast second kick would be more effective in that specific instance. Whatever the case, be versatile in the speed with which you throw so that you vary it according to your opponent's reactions at the time. Again, set up this kick with a couple of low roundhouse kicks first, getting your opponent thinking low before doubling it up on him.

2

4

5

7

8

Side Kick, Hook Kick

(1) From your fighting stance, (2) slide up to a 45-degree angle side kick position. (3) Extend your side kick out to the mid-section of your opponent, (4) rechamber your kicking leg, and immediately (5) follow up with a hook kick to the face. (6) Rechamber, and (7) return to your fighting stance. *Tips for a great kick:* This is a very effective combination. And, the transition from a fast kick to a strong kick is a beautiful display of form. Remember to change the angles from one kick to the other to make them effective —a high kick to a low kick, or vice versa. This will add to your opponent's confusion. Again, a pause in between kicks sometimes helps with the success of the technique.

2

4

5

7

1

Double Side Kick

(1) From your fighting stance, (2) slide your rear foot up directly behind your lead foot, and (3) chamber your front leg to the side kick position. (4) Execute a low side kick to the legs of your opponent; (5) rechamber your kicking leg quickly, and immediately (6) follow with a high side kick. Kick only as high as you are able to. (7) Chamber your kicking leg, and (8) settle back down to your fighting stance. *Tips for a great kick:* The double side kick is very effective in street situations. Remember that the most important quality of any double kick technique is that the kicks contrast with each other. If you know that you can't kick straight up in the air on your second kick, then aim your first kick low enough so that your follow-up high kick will be considerably higher. This sudden shift in target areas on your opponent's body is difficult to defend and enhances the effectiveness of doubling up.

3

6

Triple Side Kick

(1) From your fighting stance, (2) begin with a skip up for momentum. (3) Chamber your leg for a side kick. (4) Execute a low side kick to the leg. (5) Bring your leg

1

3

4

5

Continued

6

back up to a 45-degree angle, and (6) follow up with a side kick to the midsection. (7) Again, rechamber. (8) Finish off with a high side kick to the face. (9) Rechamber, and (10) return to your fighting stance. *Tips for a great kick:* Remember that the angles of the kicks must all contrast each other. This technique is very effective when thrown quickly, and sometimes you can change the order of the kicks. You can go: low, middle, high; or high, middle, low; or middle, high, low; etc. At the point of the high kick, you can lean back, but make sure to keep your head up and forward to keep from falling.

8

7

9

10

Slapping Hands Front Kick

This technique will help in coordinating hands and foot together, and developing the ability to judge your effective striking distance for hands and feet, especially for kick and punch combinations. (1) Begin with your feet together. (2) Take a step forward as you bring your arm of the same side as your forward leg up overhead in a motion similar to that of swimming the backstroke. (3) Circle the arm back as you step forward with the other leg and raise the other arm in the same manner. (4) Leave the raised arm in position overhead and continue to circle the other arm from back, then up in front to join the raised arm overhead. (5) Execute a front stretch with your rear leg, slapping your hands to your foot. (6-8) Lower your kicking leg as you step forward with it into a high cat stance. *Tips for a great kick:* Remember to backstroke as you step, bringing up the arm of the same side as your stepping leg. Also, your form is proper when: your hips are forward and not turned; the heel of your rear foot is always on the ground; your back is straight and not hunched. Practicing this will improve your machine gun kicks considerably.

Front Kick, Side Kick, Punch

(1) Start out in a reverse front punch extended position. As you (2&3) front kick with your back leg, simultaneously execute a front punch with the opposite arm. (4&5) Recoil your kicking leg to a side kick position, (6) execute the side kick, and simultaneously execute a front punch with the arm of the same side as your kicking leg. (7) Recoil your leg and (8) return it back to its original position as you assume a fighting stance. *Tips for a great kick:* This is an excellent technique for a form. It is very exciting to watch as well as execute. The proper timing of hand and foot techniques is sometimes difficult to accomplish in the beginning. However, the slapping hands front kick helps to develop this coordination. The most important aspect is to time your punches so they land exactly at full extension with your kicks.

Machine Gun Turret Kick

This kick is an original technique devised for form competition. (1) From your fighting stance, (2) chamber your back leg up to the roundhouse kicking position. This technique is done by turning from roundhouse to roundhouse. (3) Execute a high roundhouse kick, and as you (4) rechamber your kicking leg, pivot slightly on the ball of your foot. (5) Execute another high roundhouse, and (6-16) repeat one roundhouse after another while pivoting on the ball of your

foot. Fire your kicks rapidly as you go around in circles without stopping. You may want to do more, but these training kicks go in five to ten circles for a total of between 30 to 55 kicks before bringing the leg down. This exercise is excellent for building up stamina and strength in the quadriceps for great kicking power. Good luck.

10

12

13

15

16

BLACK BELT™ VIDEO PRESENTS

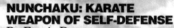

NUNCHAKU: KARATE WEAPON OF SELF-DEFENSE
By Fumio Demura
Students are taught to use the *nunchaku* in a traditional manner. Topics covered: how to grip, stances, blocking, striking, calisthenics, karate and nunchaku similarities, and whipping, applied attacking, and applied block and counter.
Code No. 1010-VHS (60 min.)

BRUCE LEE'S FIGHTING METHOD: Basic Training and Self-Defense Techniques
By Ted Wong and Richard Bustillo
Bruce Lee's *jeet kune do*, as explained in *Bruce Lee's Fighting Method*. This covers the first two volumes, with topics including warm-ups, basic exercises, on-guard position, footwork, power/speed training and self-defense.
Code No. 1020-VHS (55 min.)

TAI CHI CHUAN
By Marshall Ho'o
World expert in *tai chi chuan* teaches this Chinese practice, which promotes mind-body awareness and rejuvenation. Topics covered: the nine temple exercises, the short form, push hands and self-defense applications.
Code No. 1030-VHS (90 min.)

KARATE (SHITO-RYU)
By Fumio Demura
This program includes: warm-up exercises; an analysis of basics, including striking points, target areas, standing positions, and hand, elbow, kicking and blocking techniques; three ten-minute workouts; and a demo of basic sparring and self-defense.
Code No. 1040-VHS (90 min.)

Rainbow Publications Inc.

Mail to:
Black Belt Magazine Video
P.O. Box 918, Santa Clarita, California 91380-9018
Or Call:
Toll-Free 1(800)423-2874